POCKET PRAYERS
FOR TROUBLED
TIMES

Other books in the series:

Pocket Celtic Prayers
compiled by Martin Wallace

Pocket Graces
compiled by Pam Robertson

Pocket Prayers for Children
compiled by Christopher Herbert

Pocket Prayers: The Classic Collection
compiled by Christopher Herbert

Pocket Prayers for Advent and Christmas
compiled by Jan McFarlane

Pocket Prayers for Commuters
compiled by Christopher Herbert

Pocket Prayers for Healing and Wholeness
compiled by Trevor Lloyd

Pocket Prayers for Marriage
compiled by Andrew and Pippa Body

Pocket Prayers for Parents
compiled by Hamish and Sue Bruce

Pocket Words of Comfort
compiled by Christopher Herbert

POCKET PRAYERS
FOR TROUBLED TIMES

COMPILED BY
JOHN PRITCHARD

CHURCH HOUSE
PUBLISHING

Church House Publishing
Church House
Great Smith Street
London SW1P 3AZ

ISBN 978 0 7151 4195 3

Published 2009 by Church House Publishing

Designed by www.penguinboy.net
Printed in England by Ashford Colour Press Ltd, Fareham, Hants

CONTENTS

CONTENTS

INTRODUCTION

For all life's beauty and fascination, none of us go through life unscathed. We all bear the scars of bad experiences, whether they be of illness, unemployment, financial anxiety, damaged relationships, or even global insecurity.

In troubled times men and women have always taken these problems to God, and they have not done so in vain. Through prayer they have found the resources to cope, to handle or even to overcome those problems.

Sometimes our prayers are too deep for words, and it is then that the Holy Spirit will be interceding for us when we can't do it for ourselves (Romans 8.26). Sometimes, however, it helps to have the prayers of other people as we struggle to articulate what we feel or need.

That is what this book is for. The prayers may not exactly echo what is going on within us, but they may come close to doing so and enable us to pray more easily for ourselves. Moreover, it may be good to remember that it's all right not to know what to say and that quiet listening, and attending to our 'deep thoughts', is as important as speaking. Some people even think of prayer as simply 'thinking in the direction of God'.

A specific resource for praying in troubled times is the book of Psalms in the Old Testament. All human life is here, including a rich vein of prayer in distress. Psalms such as 6, 51, 55 and 69 all speak with fierce honesty from dark places. Those of a nervous disposition may want to brace themselves before trying Psalm 58! When we think we're alone in our desert experiences, we may well find that the psalmist is a good companion.

One thing we can be sure of is that no prayer goes unanswered, inasmuch as God will take and use every prayer to bring as much good as possible out of our situation. The bottom line is that Jesus has promised: 'I will be with you always, to the end of the age' (Matthew 28.20, TEV).

Trust him.

+John Pritchard
Bishop of Oxford

WORK, UNEMPLOYMENT AND MONEY

Work is a mixed blessing for some, but unemployment is invariably a curse. A job of work gives value to our lives and a framework to our days. It also gives us the financial security to enjoy our leisure time and to share our relative good fortune with others, as well as to know we can afford housing, holidays and hospitality.

Unemployment, on the other hand, is a dispiriting and often demeaning experience which undermines morale and can set off a spiral of decline. Life becomes difficult for everyone. We can become scratchy and irritable. Bills mount up and motivation sinks. We are poor company and may suffer low-level depression. Unemployment is bad news for the economy, for communities, for families and for individuals.

Even for those in work, the reality can be stressful and the grind of work can be enervating. The sense of being under pressure pervades society.

Prayer is no quick fix. Prayer does, however, introduce a new dimension to the unwelcome, lumpy experience of stressful work and unemployment. It provides a different back-lighting to the unpredictability of working life, a different screen-saver to our thinking. Prayer is essentially an attitude, a comprehensive way of looking at life in the light of God.

And its most common fruit is hope.

HARD TIMES

Sometimes we find ourselves caught up in major economic and financial readjustments – even global recession – and the price is paid by the employee and the homeowner, the young person looking for a first job and the middle-aged people who find they are too old to be wanted. How, then, shall we pray?

O Lord, you have searched me out and known me;
you know my sitting down and my rising up;
you discern my thoughts from afar.
You mark out my journeys and my resting place
and are acquainted with all my ways . . .
Where can I go then from your spirit?
Or where can I flee from your presence? . . .
If I take the wings of the morning
and dwell in the uttermost parts of the sea,
even there your hand shall lead me,
your right hand hold me fast.

Psalm 139.1-3,7,9-10

Lord God, we live in disturbing days:
across the world
prices rise, debts increase,
banks collapse, jobs are taken away,
and fragile security is under threat.
Loving God, meet us in our fear and hear our prayer:
be a tower of strength amidst the shifting sands,
and a light in the darkness;
help us receive your gift of peace,
and fix our hearts where true joys are to be found,
in Jesus Christ our Lord.
Church of England

You Lord are in this place,
your presence fills it,
your presence is peace.

You Lord are in my life,
your presence fills it,
your presence is peace.

You Lord are in the storm,
your presence fills it,
your presence is peace.
David Adam

'Redundant' – the word says it all –
'Useless, unnecessary,
without purpose, surplus to requirements.'

Thank you, Heavenly Father, that in the middle of
the sadness, the anger,
the uncertainty, the pain,
I can talk to you.

Hear me as I cry out in confusion,
help me to think clearly,
and calm my soul.

As life carries on,
may I know your presence with me
each and every day.

And as I look to the future,
help me to look for fresh opportunities, for new
directions.
Guide me by your Spirit,
and show me your path,

through Jesus, the way, the truth, and the life.
Church of England

God of the world, Guide of the nations,
we lay down before you the sorrows and inadequacies
of our economic and social systems.
We have trusted in credit and financial fairy tales;
we have set the markets free and watched them fail;
we have built our house on sand.
Teach us, we pray, the ancient wisdom of our faith,
that love of money for its own sake is fatal,
that debt is a snare and a delusion,
that where our treasure is, there our heart will be also.
So may we seek the better way
of honesty, humility and accountability
in the Kingdom we pray will come on earth,
as it is in heaven.

O God of comfort and challenge
whose presence is ever reliable
and ever unexpected:
grant us to grieve over what is ending
without falling into despair
and to enter our new vocation
without forgetting your voice,
through Jesus Christ. Amen.

Janet Morley

MONEY WORRIES

The first place we are hit in troubled economic times is in the pocket. Debt has become a way of life for millions of credit-card holders, for students taking out loans, for parents wanting the best for their children. But then we get caught.

God of power,
you are strong to save
and you never fail those who trust in you.
Keep under your protection
all who suffer as a result of debt:
help them through their time of darkness,
give wisdom to all who seek to help,
and bring them to know true freedom
in your Son, Jesus Christ our Lord.

Church of England

Gracious God,
you know our need of money.
'Times are hard', they say,
but harder for some than others,
harder for us, in fact.
The mortgage, the supermarket, the heating,
the car, the insurance, the council tax,
the family, the TV, the odd meal out . . .
I don't ask you for money (how could I?)
but I do ask you for more patience than I've got
and more grace than I find in my frustrated soul.
Ease your way back into my life, I pray,
and restore my sense of perspective and purpose,
for Jesus' sake, and for mine.

Lord, I'm anxious about money –
there's no getting away from it.
Please keep me sensible,
clear my head,
give me new ideas,
and help me trust in you.

Gracious God,
the world belongs to you
but we struggle to make it work.
The world's wealth is shared so unequally;
the injustice of it cries to the heavens.
Although money may be in short supply
in these hard times,
keep us in mind of the even larger problems
of the world's poor.
May our problems make us sensitive to their
problems, and their problems remind us
of our need for one another
and for you.

WORKING AT GOD'S PACE

Working life has never been more relentless for many people. The human cost of overwork, combined with stress at home and the frenetic pace of twenty-first-century existence, takes many people to the edge. That's when we need to ease back and ask ourselves more prayerful questions.

Living God,
when I am tired and cross and despairing,
distracted by many thoughts,
eaten up by multiple demands,
and hungry for your peace;
help me to offer again
the five loaves and two fishes
that you have given me,
and so discover again
the miracle of the strength
that comes in sharing everything
when we have nothing –
except Jesus Christ our Lord.

Julie M. Hulme

Lord, you put twenty-four hours in a day, and gave me
a body which gets tired and can only do so much.
Show me which tasks you want me to do, and help me
to live prayerfully as I do them.

Sharpen my senses, that I may truly
    see what I am looking at,
    taste what I am eating,
    listen to what I am hearing,
    face what I am suffering,
    celebrate the ways I am loved,
    and offer to you whatever I am doing,
so that the water of the present moment
may be turned into wine
through Jesus Christ our Lord.

Angela Ashwin

Psalm 23 for busy people

The Lord is my Pace-setter, I shall not rush,
He makes me stop and rest for quiet intervals,
He provides me with images of stillness
which restore my serenity.
He leads me in ways of efficiency,
through calmness of mind;
and his guidance is peace.
Even though I have a great many things
to accomplish each day,
I will not fret, for his presence is here.
His timelessness, his all-importance
will keep me in balance.
He prepares refreshment and renewal
in the midst of my activity,
by anointing my mind with his oils of tranquillity.
My cup of joyous energy overflows.
Surely harmony and effectiveness
shall be the fruits of my hours,
for I shall walk in the pace of my Lord,
and dwell in his house for ever.

Toki Miyashina

DRUDGERY DIVINE?

In spite of the dangers of stress and unemployment, purposeful work is a blessing. It offers dignity and satisfaction, and a framework for life. George Herbert uses the image of a 'famous stone' to illustrate the way that work, like everything else, can be redeemed and made valuable.

Teach me, my God and King,
In all things thee to see;
And what I do in anything
To do it as for thee!

All may of thee partake;
Nothing can be so mean
Which with this tincture, 'for thy sake',
Will not grow bright and clean.

A servant with this clause
Makes drudgery divine;
Who sweeps a room, as for thy laws,
Makes that and the action fine.

This is the famous stone
That turneth all to gold;
For that which God doth touch and own
Cannot for less be told.

George Herbert (1593–1633)

Jesus, Master Carpenter of Nazareth,
who on the cross through wood and nails
did work our whole salvation:
wield well your tools in this the workshop of your
world,
that we who come to you rough hewn
may by your hand be fashioned to a truer beauty
and a greater usefulness,
for the honour of your name.

Toc H

'ALL SHALL BE WELL'

When we pray in troubled economic times we can easily feel powerless, caught in a machine much larger than anything we can influence. Many prayers, therefore, take us into the heart of the heart of God where there is reassurance and hope beyond the vicissitudes of every day.

I believe I shall see the goodness of the Lord
in the land of the living.
Wait for the Lord;
be strong, and let your heart take courage;
wait for the Lord!
Psalm 27.13-14, NRSV

Lord, in these times
when we fear we are losing hope
or feel that our efforts are futile,
let us see in our hearts and minds
the image of your resurrection.
Let that be our source of courage and strength,
and with that, and in your company,
help us to face our challenges and struggles
against all that is born of despair,
through Jesus Christ our living hope.

From the Philippines

In you Lord I live,
   I move,
   I have my being.
In me Lord you live,
   you move,
   you have your being.
In this, Lord, may I find peace.

God grant me the grace to accept with serenity
the things I cannot change,
courage to change the things I can,
and wisdom to know the difference,
living one day at a time,
enjoying one moment at a time;
accepting that hardship is sometimes the way
to peace,
taking as you did this sinful world as it is,
not as I would have it;
trusting that you will make all things well
as I surrender to your will;
that I may be happy enough in this life,
and supremely happy with you in the next.

Reinhold Niebuhr (1892–1971) (adapted)

I weave into my life this day
the presence of God upon my way;
I weave into my life this hour
the mighty God and all his power;
I weave into my sore distress
his peace and calm and no less.
I weave into my step so lame
healing and help in his great name;
I weave into the darkest night
strands of God shining bright;
I weave into each deed done
joy and hope of the risen Son.

David Adam

Let nothing disturb thee,
let nothing dismay thee:
all things pass:
God never changes.
Patience attains
all that it strives for:
he who has God
finds he lacks nothing:
God alone suffices.

St Teresa of Avila (1515–82)

Our Lord spoke these words with utter certainty:
'You will not be overcome.'

The words 'You will not be overcome'
were spoken firmly to give assurance
and comfort against all the troubles that might come.

He did not say, 'You will not be tempested,
you will not be troubled,
you will not be distressed.'

He said, 'You will not be overcome.'

It is God's will that we pay attention to his words
and that we remain strong in certainty
in prosperity and trouble.
Because he loves us he wants us to love him
and trust him – and all shall be well.
Julian of Norwich (c.1342–c.1413)

HOME LIFE AND RELATIONSHIPS

Our home is sometimes our castle but also sometimes the place where we feel most insecure, most exposed and vulnerable. When all is well, home is a place to aim for. We open the front door, take in the friendly sights, smell the familiar scents, drop our bag on the floor and head for the kitchen – home! On other occasions we might go home with mounting trepidation, fearful of the tension; the first argument; the air of restrained hostility.

Our relationships have the capacity to take us higher or lower than anything else we experience. We may find ourselves loving the people we hate and hating the people we love. Is there no end to our ambivalence?

Perhaps not. But there is a place to take it and a deeper Presence to discover at the heart of our complexities. Prayer may not 'fix' our problems, but it does change both us and the emotional context of our relationships. Prayer gives God access to our over-defended lives. Prayer lets God's Spirit permeate the bone-hard ground of our confusions.

HOME LIFE

Home life is the soil out of which both joy and unhappiness may grow. Nothing is better than our home; nothing is worse. But always, God is our gracious Companion, seeking our well-being.

Gentle God,
grant that at home
where we are most truly ourselves,
where we are known at our best and our worst,
we may learn to forgive and be forgiven,
through Jesus Christ our Lord.
A New Zealand Prayer Book

God is faithful, and he will not let you be tested beyond your strength, but with the testing he will also provide the way out so that you may be able to endure it.
1 Corinthians 10.13

O God, make the door of this house wide enough
to receive all who need human love and friendship,
but narrow enough to shut out all envy,
pride and malice.
Make its threshold smooth enough to be
no stumbling block to children, nor to straying feet,
but strong enough to turn away the power of evil.
O God, make the door of this house a gateway
to your eternal kingdom.
Grant this through Christ our Lord.

Thomas Ken (1637–1711), adapted

Merciful God,
prone as we are to blame others and to hate ourselves,
take from our eyes the dust that blinds us,
that we may treat one another
by the light of your compassion,
and in the Spirit of Jesus Christ
who is the Light of the world.

Jim Cotter

Gracious God,
it hurts so much to see our children suffer;
their confusion is the deepest cut of all.
When our adult lives degenerate into chaos
unite us in determination to minimize their pain,
to maximize their security,
and to leave them in no doubt
that they are loved beyond measure.
So may they grow up confident and undamaged,
and make their relationships better than ours,
for Jesus' sake, and for theirs.

BREAKDOWN

*But then, sometimes, it happens. The final act. Separation.
We try everything to avoid this catastrophe, whether for
ourselves or for others, but sometimes a marriage dies. How
then shall we pray – for ourselves, our former partner, our
loved ones? And how shall we pray for those we know and
love who are going through the pain of breakdown?*

Hear my crying, O God,
and listen to my prayer.
From the end of the earth I call to you with fainting
heart;
O set me on the rock that is higher than I.

Psalm 61.1-2

Lord, take away this cup of bitterness.
Break my anger, as my heart has been broken.
In the darkness of my hurt, let there be hope.
And, one day, perhaps,
let there be love again.

Jane Robson

I have no wit, no words, no tears;
My heart within me like a stone
Is numbed too much for hopes or fears.
Look right, look left, I dwell alone;
I lift mine eyes, but dimmed with grief
No everlasting hills I see;
My life is in the falling leaf:
O Jesus, quicken me.

My life is like a faded leaf,
My harvest dwindled to a husk:
Truly my life is void and brief
And tedious in the barren dusk;
My life is like a frozen thing,
No bud nor greenness can I see:
Yet rise it shall – the sap of Spring;
O Jesus, rise in me.
Christina Rossetti (1830–94)

O Lord, we pray for those
who once chose a partner for life,
full of confidence and love,
and now find themselves alone.
Set their hurt and bitterness
in the liquid solution of your grace.
Bind them up and hold them as a parent holds a child.
May yours be the hands that set them on their feet
and yours the eyes that smile them into life,
so that, eventually,
all shall be well, and all manner of things shall be well.

Faithful God,
many people feel diminished by this ending.
Some will not be reconciled to it,
and many will grieve.
Be their comfort and support,
and allow them to face this new life
with hope for their future,
in the name of Christ.

Jeremy Fletcher

Steadfast Lover of my soul,
stay close to me today, in this season of endings,
before new chapters open.
Stay in my hands as I tidy up or pack away.
May I treasure the memories and trust my
achievements.
Stay in my feet as I close the door
and walk away for a little or forever.
Stay in my arms as I embrace those
who have shared this chapter with me.
Stay in the salty cleansing of my tears
when I say goodbye.
May I let the grieving come because I have loved here.
May I lay down any tensions now,
not forget the kindness
and celebrate the time we had together.
Stay in my heart when I feel sorrow for any failure.
May I learn from my mistakes,
accept your forgiveness and let go.
May I offer my sense of incompleteness
and imperfection.
Steadfast One, be in my eyes this day
as I look ahead to new possibilities.

Tess Ward (adapted)

BRINGING UP CHILDREN

Parents are almost inevitably on a collision course with their children at some point in their upbringing. What then do we need to ride the wave?

O God of love and mercy, help us to understand our children as they grow in years and in knowledge of your world. Make us compassionate for their temptations and failures, and encouraging in their seeking after truth and value for their lives. Stir up in us appreciation for their ideals and sympathy for their frustrations; that with them we may look for a better world than either we or they have known, through Jesus Christ, our common Lord and Master.

Massey Hamilton Shepherd Jnr

Lord, what have we done wrong?
How has our curly-haired, chubby child
become a monster?
How did our relationship degrade
from smiles and laughter
to curled lip and monosyllables?
How did we get cut off from his world
and displaced to the servants' quarters?

Graceful and consistent God,
hold us steady in the quicksands of blame and grief
and haul us out onto the far shores of hope.
Be the rock on which we rebuild our family,
emulating your patience and endless forgiveness.

And in the meantime –
help!

FRACTURED FRIENDSHIPS

One of our saddest experiences is old friendships that go sour. There is hurt, bewilderment and regret. There can also be prayer.

Dear God,
Lover of us all,
do not let me go down into the grave
with old broken friendships unresolved.
Give to us, and to all with whom
we have shared our lives and deepest selves
along the Way,
the courage not only to express anger
when we feel let down,
but your more generous love
which always seeks to reconcile
and so to build a more enduring love
between those we have held dear
as friends.
Kathy Keay

Our relationships are lived out in choppy water. Sometimes a simple image goes to the heart of our needs when we pray.

O Jesus,
Be the canoe that holds us in the sea of life.
Be the steer that keeps us on the straight course.
Be the outrigger that supports us
in times of great temptation.
Let your Spirit be our sail
that carries us through each day.
Keep our bodies strong,
so that we can paddle steadfastly on,
in the long voyage of life.
From Melanesia (adapted)

OUR BROKEN WORLD

We are surrounded all the time by wars and rumours of wars. But, as Jesus tells us, 'the end is not yet'.

As we listen to the news, the violence and fragmentation of the world is a constant shock to our innocence. Outrage is heaped upon outrage. A family of nine is wiped out in a rocket attack. A father loses his wife and three children in a conflict that is none of his doing. A young father is murdered at a bus-stop in front of his three-year-old daughter as he goes to hospital to visit his wife and newly born child. We hear of unimaginable tragedy and we may be tempted to despair.

On top of that is the daily struggle and grinding poverty of a billion people who live on less than a dollar a day, and the tragic inequality of access to clean water, health care, education and opportunity. The result is a world of aching injustice.

Prayer cannot undo the evil; it can, however, be part of the redeeming of it. We bring to God the awful wounds of the world in order to focus his love and ours on the victims and the situations in which they are caught. Such love is not a sentimental sticking plaster but the powerful and effective means by which God is healing his world in readiness for the new creation, 'a new heaven and a new earth'. This kingdom may be a long time coming, but it's unstoppable.

As Archbishop Desmond Tutu said: 'Don't give up. Don't be discouraged. I've read the end of the book. We win!'

A WORLD AT WAR

We look out on a world of violence. Only belief in something bigger than all the madness of humankind can give us some perspective and keep us in hope.

O God
it is your will to hold both heaven and earth
in a single peace.
Let the design of your great love
shine on the waste of our wraths and sorrows,
and give peace to your Church,
peace among nations,
peace in our homes,
and peace in our hearts.

A New Zealand Prayer Book

O God, compassionate and merciful,
where your children tear each other
you also are torn.
Full of confusion, longing for peace,
we bring you our violent world,
where the poorest pay the cost
of powerful hatreds.
In this time of need,
open our hearts and minds to your will,
and show us how to pray.

Janet Morley

Almighty Father,
whose will is to restore all things
in your beloved Son, the King of all:
govern the hearts and minds of those in authority,
and bring the families of the nations,
divided and torn apart by the ravages of sin,
to be subject to his just and gentle rule,
through Jesus Christ our Lord.

Common Worship

Almighty God,
in a world where naked ambition
robs others of their rights and dignity,
and gross self-interest
allows so many to bleed to death,
grant us the Spirit of your Son
that we may confront the systems
by which we live at the expense of others,
so that all who long for you
may find justice, healing and peace.

Compassionate God and Father of all,
we are horrified at the rise of terrorism
in so many parts of the world.
It seems that none are safe, and some are terrified.
The world seems now a different place
from the one we grew up in.

Hold back the hands that kill and maim;
turn around the hearts that hate.
Grant instead your strong Spirit of peace –
peace that passes our understanding
but changes lives,
through Jesus Christ our Lord.

PEACEMAKERS

The search for peace is a human task, not one we can
simply project onto God. We need to pray for our national
leaders, recognizing the high price they pay in responsibility
and accountability, not only to us but to the future.

Eternal God, Fount of wisdom,
we ask you to bless the national leaders
we have elected;
grant that through their discussions and decisions
we may solve our problems effectively,
enhance the well-being of our nation,
and achieve together a fairer and more united society.
A New Zealand Prayer Book (adapted)

Dear Lord,
give us new prophets who can speak openly,
directly, convincingly, and lovingly
to kings, presidents, religious leaders,
and all men and women of good will,
prophets who can make us wage peace instead of war.
Lord, make haste to help us.
Do not come too late!
Henri Nouwen

OUR RESPONSIBILITIES

Behind our leaders are the irreducible complexities of our own hearts. The search for peace starts in the examination of our own motives and sometimes dark desires.

The hatred which divides nation from nation,
race from race, class from class,
Father, forgive.

The covetous desires of people and nations
to possess what is not their own,
Father, forgive.

The greed which exploits the labours
of men and women,
and lays waste the earth,
Father, forgive.

Our envy of the welfare and happiness of others,
Father, forgive.

Our indifference to the plight of the homeless
and the refugee,
Father, forgive.

The lust which uses for ignoble ends
the bodies of men and women,
Father, forgive.

The pride which leads us to trust in ourselves
and not in God,
Father, forgive.

Anon, written on the altar of Coventry Cathedral

Show us, good Lord,
the peace we should seek,
the peace we must give,
the peace we can keep,
the peace we must forgo,
and the peace you have given
in Jesus Christ our Lord.

**Caryl Micklem; used by the Corrymeela Community in Northern
Ireland**

Lord, we pray for peace,
not peace at any price
but peace at your price.
Make us and all your children so rich with your love,
your generosity, your justice,
that we can afford to pay the cost of your peace.
Mothers' Union

FOUR MAJOR ISSUES

There are particular sorrows that call for our prayers. Four named here are inequality, hunger, the forces that create refugees and the destructiveness of landmines.

Let justice roll down like waters,
And righteousness like an ever-flowing stream.
Amos 5.24

Here is a gaping sore, Lord:
Half the world diets,
the other half hungers.
Half the world is housed,
the other half is homeless.
Half the world pursues profit,
the other half senses loss.
Redeem our souls,
redeem our peoples,
redeem our times.

John Bell

O God, who created us out of love,
we pray for all who are destitute and without hope.
Help us to understand what it's like to be poor or
marginalized,
to have no clean water,
or to be exhausted by the sheer struggle to survive.
Fire our imaginations,
and empower us to work for the relief of their
suffering,
and the shaping of a better world,
through Jesus Christ our Lord. Amen.

Angela Ashwin (adapted)

Lord God, we pray for all the bombed out,
burned out,
driven out, relocated, wondering,
wandering, sorrowing,
unwilling pilgrims in this world.
Forgive us for our part in uprooting them,
restore their lives,
assist your Church to be partners with them
in the rebuilding of their lives.
We pray in the name of the Son of Man,
who had no place to lay his head.

Arnold Kenseth and Richard Unsworth (adapted)

'Lord, how can I serve you without arms?
How can I walk in your way without feet?
I was collecting sticks for the fire when I lost my arms.
I was taking the goats to water when I lost my feet.
I have a head but my head does not understand
why there are landmines
in the grazing land or why there is a tripwire
across the dusty road
to the market.'

My heart is filled with a long ache.
I want to share your pain but I cannot.

It is too deep for me.
You look at me but I cannot bear your gaze.
The arms factory provides a job for my son
and my taxes paid for the
development of smart bombs.
I did not protest when the soldiers planted fear
into the earth
that smothers the old people and the anxious mothers
and fills the young men with hate.

Lord, we are all accomplices in the crime of war,
which is a lust for power
at all costs.
The cost is too much for humanity to bear.
Lord, give us back our humanity, our ubuntu . . .
Teach us to serve you without arms.

Archbishop Desmond Tutu

What does the Lord require of you
but to do justice,
and to love kindness,
and to walk humbly with your God?

Micah 6.8

SEEING CHRIST

*Christians are called to find Jesus in the faces of the poor.
It's not easy, but it's the first step towards compassionate
action.*

Christ, let me see you in others.
Christ, let others see you in me.
Christ, let me see:

You are the caller
You are the poor
You are the stranger at my door.

You are the wanderer
The unfed
You are the homeless
With no bed.

You are the man
Driven insane
You are the child
Crying in pain

You are the other who comes to me
Open my eyes that I may see.

David Adam

LORD OF ALL HOPEFULNESS

The final word for a believer will always be one of hope.

Eternal God,
in whose perfect realm
no sword is drawn but the sword of righteousness,
and no strength known but the strength of love:
so guide and inspire the work of those
who seek your kingdom
that all your people may find their security
in that love which casts out fear
and in the fellowship revealed to us
in Jesus Christ our Saviour.

Common Worship

Creator God,
Give us a heart for simple things:
    love and laughter
    bread and wine
    tales and dreams.
Fill our lives
with green and growing hope;
make us a people of justice
whose song is Alleluiah
and whose name breathes love.
From South Africa

The wolf shall live with the lamb,
  the leopard shall lie down with the kid,
  the calf and the lion and the fatling together,
  and a little child shall lead them . . .
They will not hurt or destroy
  on all my holy mountain;
  for the earth will be full
  of the knowledge of the Lord,
  as the waters cover the sea.
Isaiah 11.6,9

OUR FRAGILE EARTH

The statistics frighten us. All around are signs of the degradation of the earth on which we depend. Ice packs are melting, seas are rising, forests are disappearing, species are vanishing, deserts are growing, populations are moving, crops are failing, fresh water is becoming a precious commodity, the world is becoming an ever more unequal place. Who will save us?

The answer is that we have to save ourselves. Governments have to respond to the cry of the people that we cannot continue to consume in the rampant, thoughtless way we have done throughout the industrial age. Enough really is enough.

However, people of faith call on other resources for personal and social change. They call on God to inspire and motivate all those of good will to activate those levers of change which engage both the human heart and political will. In that sense, who can save us but God?

Our prayer, however, is best if it is not obsessed with disaster but flows from a grateful and appreciative heart. 'The heavens are telling the glory of God; and the firmament declares his handiwork' (Psalm 19.1). From that joy in creation may come our determination to preserve it.

THE JOY OF THE EARTH

God of the high and holy places
where I catch a glimpse of your glory,
above the low levels of life,
above the evil and emptiness that drags me down,
beyond the limits of my senses and imagination,
you lift me up.

In the splendour of a sunset,
in the silence of the stars,
in the grandeur of the mountains,
in the vastness of the sea,
you lift me up.

In the majesty of music,
in the mystery of art,
in the freshness of the morning,
in the fragrance of a single flower,
you lift me up.

Jean Mortimer

O Lord, how manifold are your works!
In wisdom you have made them all;
the earth is full of your creatures.
Yonder is the sea, great and wide,
creeping things innumerable are there,
living things both small and great.
There go the ships,
and Leviathan that you formed to sport in it.
These all look to you
to give them their food in due season;
when you give to them, they gather it up;
when you open your hand, they are filled with good
things.
When you hide your face, they are dismayed;
when you take away their breath, they die
and return to the dust.
When you send forth your spirit, they are created;
and you renew the face of the ground.
May the glory of the Lord endure for ever;
May the Lord rejoice in his works.

Psalm 104.24-31, NRSV

EARTH-ABUSE

*Nevertheless, we have to move from gratitude to penitence,
for we have abused our privilege as stewards and co-
creators of this good earth. This is not breast-beating but
honesty, and it prepares the ground for positive prayer and
action.*

God of creation, the earth is yours
with all its beauty and goodness,
its rich and overflowing provision.

But we have claimed it for our own,
plundered its beauty for profit,
and grabbed its resources for ourselves.

God of creation, forgive us.
May we no longer abuse your trust,
but care gently and with justice for your earth.

Jan Berry

Father, we confess that we have been blind
to how our lives impact others,
and especially the poorest communities.
We confess that we have taken the earth for granted,
using fossil fuels without a second thought
and failing to recognize our part
in the problem of climate change.
We turn back to you
and ask you to help us to live simpler lives
and to be much more careful
with all the resources we have
– because it is your earth.
Christian Concern for One World

Forgive us, God,
that we have taken your creation for granted.
You have given us
the run of the land,
the pick of the crop,
and we have squandered these resources;
distributed them unfairly,
vandalized their beauty,
violated their purity.

Forgive us, God,
that we have taken your kingdom for granted.
You have given us
the seeds of faith,
the fruits of the spirit,
and we have misused these resources;
displayed them rarely,
bestowed them grudgingly,
ignored them blithely.

Thank you, God,
that you are stronger than our destructiveness
and greater than our meanness,
and that you give us a fresh start and a second chance.
Lead us in the conquest of our own greed,
and drive us towards a new life
of justice, peace and the integrity of creation.

Jean Mortimer (adapted)

SUSTAINING THE EARTH

Out of our penitence should come our resolve to serve and save the earth. Well-worded prayers are not enough, of course, but they should lead us to committed action.

Eternal Father, source of life and light,
whose love extends to all people,
all creatures, all things:
grant us that reverence for life
which becomes those who believe in you;
lest we despise it, degrade it,
or come callously to destroy it.
Rather let us save it, serve it, and sanctify it,
after the example of your Son, Jesus Christ our Lord.

Robert Runcie

Loving Lord God,
show us how to do things well today,
so that others may not suffer,
here or there,
now or in the future.
Show us how to make our contribution
as we change the way we live, travel,
make and consume, pack and unpack,
use, misuse and re-use energy, heating and lighting.
Show us how to do simple things well in our homes,
our places of work and our lifestyle choices.
Show us how to protect the world you made,
in all its diversity and goodness,
from our carbon emissions,
global warming and climate change,
rising temperatures and sea levels,
displacement of peoples, environmental poverty,
harm and destruction.
Show us how and tell us why,
so that alone and with others
our contribution will make a difference.

Robin Morrison

God our creator,
you have made us one with this earth,
to tend it and to bring forth fruit;
may we so respect and cherish
all that has life from you,
that we may share in the labour of all creation
to give birth to your hidden glory,
through Jesus Christ.
Janet Morley

Jesus Christ,
in changing weather, vanishing species,
and impoverished neighbours,
the heavens and the earth bear witness against us.
As you lit an Easter fire
and cooked breakfast by the lakeside,
fashioning God's kingdom from the stuff of the earth,
so, when we cook and light and warm our homes,
make us people of your resurrection,
choosing life
through simplicity, ingenuity and obedience.
Eleanor Todd (adapted)

Show us, O God, how to love not only animals, birds
and all green and growing things, but the soil, air and
water by which we live, so that we may not exploit or
pollute them for our own profit or convenience.
Help us to cherish these necessities for our survival,
and guide those in authority to ensure that the human
spirit may not be starved in pursuit of material
comfort and wealth.
Through Jesus Christ our Lord.

Phoebe Hesketh

Come to the waters, all you who are thirsty:
children who need water free from diseases,
women who need respite from labour and searching,
plants that need moisture rooted near the bedrock,
find here a living spring.
O God, may we thirst for your waters of justice,
and learn to deny no-one the water of life.

Christian Aid

NOT STATISTICS BUT PEOPLE

Never let us forget the human cost of our playing with a fragile earth. Here is a prayer written by young people in Kenya.

We pray for people so poor
that they cannot help themselves;
whose subsistence crops
have been destroyed by climatic disasters;
for people who live in areas
where rainfall is unreliable
and varies from year to year.
We pray for small children
who die of malnutrition,
and others who suffer from disease
because their mothers do not understand
the values of different kinds of foods.
We pray for little children,
too young
to pray for themselves.

BLESSING

A Gaelic blessing and a biblical promise.

May the road rise to meet you.
May the wind be always at your back.
May the sun shine warm upon your face.
May the rains fall softly upon your fields
    until we meet again.
May God hold you in the hollow of his hand.

For the creation waits with eager longing for the
revealing of the children of God; for . . . the creation
itself will be set free from its bondage to decay and
will obtain the freedom of the glory of the children of
God. We know that the whole creation has been
groaning in labour pains until now.
Romans 8.19,21-22

IN TIMES OF ILLNESS

Illness takes us down. Whether it be in us or in ones we deeply love, illness exposes the fragility of our hold on life. We hope; we bargain; we despair; we hope again. We feel angry, lonely, depressed, afraid. Above all, perhaps, we feel bewildered. Life was going along fine, and suddenly all the familiar landmarks have shifted; the reassuring routines are in disarray.

And yet the rest of the world carries on as if nothing has changed. Don't they know that everything is different? Don't they feel the chill of fear? How can they laugh, and smile, and plan what to do at the weekend?

Christians have another resource at these times of confusion. They can take their bundle of ragged emotions and drop them into God's capacious keeping. They don't look for magic solutions, but they do look for the many gifts God brings to this darkness. They look for patience, strength, understanding; the healing activity of God in their minds and bodies and in the skill of medical staff. Above all, they look for divine companionship so they know they are not alone.

Illness catches us off guard. Prayer is a great stabilizer.

WHEN ILLNESS STRIKES

Our first response on hearing of serious illness is easily one of panic. That's entirely natural, but Jesus kept on saying in the Gospels, 'Do not be afraid.'

God of every moment,
of times of disaster and times of elation,
you enter our bewilderment and outrage;
you stand with your beautiful, broken people
in their illness and sadness.
Stay with us in our fear and confusion,
sustain us in the bleak hinterland of our loneliness
and promise us, we pray, a life beyond pain
and hope of a new day.

God who in Jesus stills the storm
and soothes the frantic heart,
bring hope and courage to . . . as he/she waits in
uncertainty.
Make him/her equal to whatever lies ahead.
Give him/her courage to endure what cannot be
avoided,
for your will is health and wholeness;
you are God and we need you.
A New Zealand Prayer Book (adapted)

Risen Lord,
when many of our fellow-citizens
succumb to illness at the same time,
you are there, standing in the midst.
We easily panic – or else unreasonably feel
it will never happen to us.
Be the rock in our turbulence, the calm in our storm,
and strengthen those who give their skill and care
to return us to health and well-being.
Through him who is always the resurrection
and the life,
Jesus Christ our Lord.

FOR THE SICK AND THOSE WHO CARE FOR THEM

After the shock comes the steady prayer, both for those who are ill and for the medical staff caring for them. Perhaps our prayer broadens out to encompass more people than just our own.

Jesus our Healer,
we place in your gentle hands those who are sick.
Ease their pain,
and heal the damage done to them
in body, mind or spirit.
Be present to them through the support of friends
and in the care of doctors and medical staff,
and fill them with the reassurance of your love
now and always.

Angela Ashwin (adapted)

Lord God, whose Son, Jesus Christ,
understood people's fear and pain
before they spoke of them,
we pray for those in hospital;
surround the frightened with your tenderness;
give strength to those in pain;
hold the weak in your arms of love,
and give hope and patience
to those who are recovering;
we ask this through the same Jesus Christ, our Lord.
Christine McMullen

God of grace and compassion,
we salute those who seek to heal
our wounds and worries.
We give thanks for the gentle touch of medical staff
in the lives and problems of thousands this day,
bringing confidence and comfort
to spirits disabled by fear.
Bless them with gifts beyond themselves,
and sustain them
with love that brooks no compromise
and has no end,
for it flows from the Source of Love himself,
Jesus Christ our Lord.

That evening, at sunset, they brought to him all who were sick or possessed with demons. And the whole city was gathered around the door. And he cured many who were sick with various diseases.

Mark 1.32-34

CHALLENGE TO FAITH

Illness is a great sifter of faith. Sometimes we are strengthened in faith; sometimes faith melts away. The greatest rewards come to those who hang in there, trusting in God inside, around and beyond the crisis of health. But sometimes the cost is high . . .

As the rain hides the stars,
as the autumn mist hides the hills,
as the clouds veil the blue of the sky,
so the dark happenings of my lot
hide the shining of your face.
Yet, if I may hold your hand in the darkness,
it is enough.
Since I know that, though I may stumble in my going,
you do not fall.

Celtic prayer

Lord, I believe; help with my unbelief,
for I believe in your deep love and mercy,
in your forgiving understanding
of the human heart.
Through the lonely watches of the spirit's night,
within the narrow tunnel of my grief,
I know a quiet dawn will come.
Tortured alone in the creeping loathsome dark
and dragged along a labyrinthine maze,
I still believe your healing sun
will bring the birth of some new day
to break the iron gates of pain,
to bring again life where hopes, broken, lie
crippled among her ancient battlements;
Lord, I believe that there will surely be light
after the midnight turns to death.

Randle Manwaring

STAYING OPEN

Those who are ill are often unable to pray much for themselves. Prayer can be reduced to a simple openness to the presence and love of God. God does the rest.

Healing love of Jesus,
fall afresh on me.
Healing love of Jesus,
fall afresh on me.
Touch me, stir me, unfold me, hold me,
Healing love of Jesus,
fall afresh on me.

Lord,
you said so gently, so persistently,
'Give me your weariness
and I'll give you my rest.'
I did – finally.
You did – immediately.
Then, Lord, I marvelled
that I had waited so long.
Ruth Harms Calkin

BEATITUDES FOR DISABLED PEOPLE

Disabled people often face long imprisonment, not helped by the misunderstanding of others. Society's awareness is growing, but there is need for more 'blessedness' in the experience of disabled people.

Blessed are you who take time to listen
to defective speech,
for you help us to know that if we persevere,
we can be understood.

Blessed are you who walk with us in public places
and ignore the stares of strangers,
for in your companionship
we find havens of relaxation.

Blessed are you who never bid us 'hurry up',
and more blessed are you who do not snatch our tasks
from our hands to do them for us,
for often we need time rather than help.

Blessed are you who stand beside us
as we enter new ventures,
for our failures will be outweighed
by times we surprise ourselves,
and you.

Blessed are you who ask for our help,
for our greatest need is to be needed.

Blessed are you
when by all of these things you assure us
that the thing that makes us individuals
is not our peculiar muscles,
nor our wounded nervous system
but is the God-given self
that no infirmity can confine.

Marjorie Chappell

DEMENTIA

Dear God,
this sorrow is too much,
losing a loved one by inches,
watching the mind grow cloudy,
taking leave of memory,
laying aside shared lives.
This is a terrible journey into oblivion.
Remind us that a person's value lies
not in what they can do,
but in who they are, made in your image.

Give us love beyond our tiredness,
patience beyond our frustration,
and hope beyond our despair.
Help us never to give up
as you draw all people into your new creation,
pre-figured in Jesus Christ our Lord.

MENTAL ILLNESS

Mental illness is one of the most troubling ailments to a society that is not at peace with itself. People are embarrassed and afraid, probably without consciously recognizing how close we all are to some experience of mental illness. Prayer is one way of sensitizing us to the needs of those who live in this lonely place.

God of endless compassion and mercy,
we come before you in sorrow
for the way we shy away
from those whose minds are confused
and full of disturbing images.
Forgive us,
for many of us will experience mental illness,
and none of us is wholly well.
We lack judgement and maturity.
we prioritize the trivial and choose harmful addictions.
Our name is Legion.
May we draw from you compassion, tenderness,
and patience,
and pass it on generously to those
who struggle with inner demons.

So may Legion be released
and enjoy the glorious freedom of the children of
God.

*('Legion' refers to the name given to the man with mental
illness whom Jesus set free by the lake in Gadara in Mark 5.)*

TRUST

*Behind and beyond the particular contours of our illnesses
is the possibility of a deep trust in God, who is always 'on
our side', willing our well-ness and empowering our body's
drive for health. Trust is a great healer.*

Be present, O merciful God, and protect us
through the silent hours of this night,
so that we who are wearied
by the changes and chances
of this fleeting world
may repose upon your eternal changelessness,
through Jesus Christ our Lord.

Gelasian Sacramentary (seventh century)

Watch thou, O Lord,
with those who wake or watch or weep tonight,
and give thine angels charge over those who sleep.
Tend thy sick ones, O Lord Christ;
rest thy weary ones; bless thy dying ones;
soothe thy suffering ones; pity thine afflicted ones;
shield thy joyous ones,
and all for thy love's sake.

St Augustine of Hippo (354–430)

Then the eyes of the blind shall be opened,
and the ears of the deaf unstopped;
then the lame shall leap like a deer,
and the tongue of the speechless sing for joy.
For waters shall break forth in the wilderness,
and streams in the desert.

Isaiah 35.6-7

IN TIMES OF BEREAVEMENT

The loss of one we truly love is the ultimate test. We ache, physically and emotionally. Life is uniformly bleak and the only horizon is grey upon grey. Our spiritual resources are stretched to breaking point. We don't think we'll ever recover.

Prayer in such circumstances often shuts down along with everything else. It's too much effort, and we may well be angry with God in any case. Nevertheless, another voice tells us that God is the only One big enough to hold such a catastrophe, and we need him as never before.

This is where the prayers of others can come to the rescue. No death is quite like any other in the history of the world, but there is sufficient of a family likeness in the experience for the words of others to speak for us. Then, perhaps, numbness, anger, depression and sad acceptance may yield finally to hope of a new world and everlasting joy.

DESOLATION

Bereavement is a lonely journey with no blueprint. Each person is a pioneer. For some, therefore, the following prayer may have no resonance, but for others it will speak of a time of deep anger and many pointed questions.

My God,
why have you let this happen?
Why did you forsake us?
Creator – why uncreate?
Redeemer – why destroy wholeness?
Source of love – why rip away
the one I loved so utterly?
Why?

In this pit of darkness,
hollowed out by grief,
I reach out to the one I loved
and cannot touch.

Where are you, God?
Where are you,
except here, in my wounds
which are also yours.

God, as I hurl at you
my aching rage and bitterness,
hold me,
and stay here
until this hacked-off stump of my life
discovers greenness again.
Angela Ashwin

LETTING GO

*The ongoing task is to let go. It happens many times: at the
point of death; at the registration of death; at the funeral;
and then every day.*

'Now, Lord, you let your servant depart in peace,
according to your word,
for my eyes have seen your salvation.'
Luke 2.29-30

O God who brought us to birth,
and in whose arms we die:
in our grief and shock
contain and comfort us;
embrace us with your love,
give us hope in our confusion,
and grace to let go into new life,
through Jesus Christ.

Janet Morley

As I rise up this morning
I remember the love that I lost.
I remember their laughter and smile,
their quirks and silly moments.
I remember the place they always sat
and the things that they once said.
I remember that old thing they used to wear
that carried their smell,
and I remember burying my head in it and weeping.
I remember with sorrow the words left unspoken,
the plans forever shelved.
And I remember the first birthdays
and the first seasons without them,
the wrongness of them leaving me here,
as the world kept turning.

And now it seems forever autumn,
the vapours and mists,
the brownness of decay,
the intractable darkness of the afternoons.
But though I can no longer touch,
time cannot undo or unravel their mark,
and I weave their love as I wend my way,
plaiting it with new love.
They are never far: in the lash of the wind,
in the birds that keep song,
in the lamp-lit streets at night,
and in the quiet of my prayer this morn,
for though the summer has gone now,
I know that spring will come.

Tess Ward (adapted)

FAREWELL

Formal farewells can sometimes carry us through the fragile transition from 'life with' to 'life without'. Here is a classic farewell, and two contemporary versions.

Go forth upon your journey from this world
O Christian soul
in the peace of him in whom you have believed,
in the name of God the Father who created you,
in the name of Jesus Christ who suffered for you,
in the name of the Holy Spirit who strengthened you.
May angels and archangels, and all the armies
of the heavenly host, come to meet you;
may all the saints of God welcome you,
may your portion this day be in gladness and peace,
and your dwelling in Paradise.
Go forth upon your journey, O Christian soul.

Commendation of a soul, Western Rite

Into the darkness and warmth of the earth
we lay you down.
Into the sadness and smiles of our memories
we lay you down.
Into the cycle of living and dying and rising again
we lay you down.
May you rest in peace, in fulfilment, in loving.
May you run straight home into God's embrace.
We love you, we miss you, we want you to be happy.
Go safely, go dancing, go running home.

Ruth Burgess

This time is for stillness.
Let us be still.
. . . , you are still after a long, hard journey.
What has happened, has happened.
What has not happened has not happened.
Let it be.
This time is quiet.
Let the quietness of peace enfold you,
all dear to you,
and all who have no peace.
And you, dear . . . , whom we love,
for you there are no more troubles and no more
sorrows.
You have laid your burden down now.
May you rest in peace.
Tess Ward

HOPE

Christians believe that death is the full stop at the end of the chapter, but that God then starts a new chapter in our lives. The distinctive gift of the Christian faith in the face of death is this golden light pouring towards us from the future. Too much light too soon may not be helpful for someone in the deep darkness of recent loss, but at the right time light may begin to seep over the horizon.

We remember, Lord, the slenderness of the thread
which separates life from death,
and the suddenness with which it can be broken.
Help us also to remember
that on both sides of that division
we are surrounded by your love.
Persuade our hearts that when our dear ones die
neither we nor they are parted from you.
In you may we find our peace and in you
be united with them in the glorious body of Christ,
who has burst the bonds of death
and is alive for evermore,
our Saviour and theirs for ever and ever.
Dick Williams

Christ is the morning star who
when the darkness of the world is past
brings to his saints
the promise of the light of life
and opens everlasting day.

The Venerable Bede (c.673–735)

OUR FUTURE

Death always brings us up against our own mortality.
Before we bury the rawness of that awkward question, the
Christian tradition assures us of a future and a hope as we
respond to the invitation of Love.

Bring us, O Lord, at our last awakening
into the house and gate of heaven,
to enter into that gate and dwell in that house
where shall be no darkness nor dazzling,
but one equal light;
no noise nor silence, but one equal music;
no fears nor hopes, but one equal possession;
no ends nor beginnings, but one equal eternity
in the habitations of your glory and dominion,
world without end.

John Donne (c.1572–1631)

O Lord, support us all the day long
of this troublous life, until the shades
lengthen, the evening comes, the busy
world is hushed, the fever of life is over,
and our work is done. Then, Lord, in
your mercy grant us safe lodging, a holy
rest, and peace at the last,
through Jesus Christ our Lord.

John Henry Newman (1801–90)

Who will separate us from the love of Christ?
... I am convinced that neither death, nor life,
nor angels, nor rulers,
nor things present, nor things to come,
nor powers, nor height, nor depth,
nor anything else in all creation,
will be able to separate us from the love of God
in Christ Jesus our Lord.

Romans 8.35,38-39

INTO GOD'S HANDS

Prayer in times of trouble isn't simply whistling in the dark, nor is it an unresolved argument with God. The end point is a quiet trust that we are always held in the hands of a love that is both extraordinary and inexhaustible. We can never slip out of that love. Everything that happens is known and shared, and God will use whatever comes to us as grist for his next action in our lives. It's called redemption.

To cast ourselves onto God in quiet trust isn't fatalism. It's based on a knowledge of the ways of God as we have seen them in the life of Jesus. Jesus never promised his followers a quiet life. He never offered a life of security and success. How could we expect an easy passage when we follow a man who died on a miserable cross?

What Jesus promised in the roller-coaster of life was his friendship, the love of his Father, and the unending support of his Spirit. St Paul, after him, promised that God 'will not let you be tested beyond your strength, but with the testing he will also provide the way out so that you may be able to endure it' (1 Corinthians 10.13). He also found that God said to him in his trials, 'My grace is sufficient for you, for my power is made perfect in weakness' (2 Corinthians 12.9).

The challenge for us is to live in and out of that confidence.

And to believe in resurrection.

COMMITMENT

Problems usually lead us to tighten our grip on everything we hope we can 'fix' for ourselves. It takes quite a lot of courage (or desperation) to make us cast everything onto God. It challenges our faith to the limit, but it opens up limitless possibilities.

'I believe; help my unbelief!'
Mark 9.24

'Father, into your hands I commend my spirit.'
Luke 23.46

Into your hands,
Lord, I commit my spirit;
into your hands,
the open and defenceless hands of love,
into your hands,
the accepting and welcoming hands of love,
into your hands,
the firm and reliable hands of love,
I commit my spirit.

Rex Chapman

I am no longer my own, but yours.
Put me to what you will, rank me with whom you will.
Put me to doing, put me to suffering:
Let me be employed for you, or laid aside for you:
Exalted for you, or brought low for you:
Let me be full, let me be empty:
Let me have all things, let me have nothing.
I freely and wholeheartedly yield all things
to your pleasure and disposal.
And now, glorious and blessed God,
Father, Son and Holy Spirit,
You are mine and I am yours. So be it.
And the covenant now made on earth,
Let it be ratified in heaven.

The Methodist Covenant, 1755

MOVING ON

Faith means that what may seem to be the end, never is.
The resurrection is our promise that God is never defeated.
God is endlessly innovative and imaginative, and the
pilgrimage goes on.

May almighty God
graciously direct you on your journey,
and bring you in safety to the place
where you wish to go,
for his merciful love is known in all places
and he treats his family with tender kindness.

May a band of angels go with you
and prepare the way before you;
may their comfort sustain you
and protect your path from harm.

May Christ who is the Way, the Truth and the Life
be your companion;
may you follow the way of justice
and reach the reward of everlasting joy.

Anon.

Pilgrim God, bless us with courage
where our way is fraught with danger.
Bless us with good companions
where the way demands a common cause.
Bless us with good humour, for we
cannot travel lightly when weighed down
with over-much solemnity.
Bless us with humility to learn from those around us.
Bless us with decisiveness
when we have to move quickly.
Bless our lazy moments, when we need to
stretch our limbs for the journey.
Bless us, lead us, love us, and bring us
home, bearing the gospel of life.

Anon.

GOD'S BLESSING

Christians are those who know they have been blessed by God and want to be a blessing to others.

God the Sender, send us.
God the Sent, come with us.
God the Strengthener of those who go,
empower us, that we may go
forever and wherever, with you,
Father, Son and Holy Spirit.

The Church in Wales

THE DESTINATION

All shall be Amen and Alleluia.
We shall rest and we shall see.
We shall see and we shall know.
We shall know and we shall love.
We shall love and we shall praise.
Behold our end which is no end.

St Augustine of Hippo (354–430)

INDEX OF FIRST LINES

INDEX OF AUTHORS AND SOURCES

ACKNOWLEDGEMENTS

The compiler and publisher gratefully acknowledge permission to reproduce copyright material in this anthology. Every effort has been made to trace and contact the copyright holders. If there are any inadvertent omissions we apologize to those concerned; please send any information to the publisher who will make a full acknowledgement in future editions.

The Archbishops' Council of the Church of England: from *Common Worship: Services and Prayers for the Church of England*, Church House Publishing 2000, (pp. 35, 45); *The Common Worship Psalter* (pp. 2, 24); prayers from the Church of England web site (www.cofe.anglican.org.uk) (pp. 4, 5, 7), copyright The Archbishops' Council, 2000, 2009.

The Anglican Church in Aotearoa, New Zealand and Polynesia: from *A New Zealand Prayer Book – He Karikia Mihinare O Aotearoa*, copyright © The Church of the Province of New Zealand, 1989 (pp. 21, 34, 37, 61).

Cairns Publications: from Jim Cotter, *Through Desert Places*, 1989; Out of the Silence, 2006; reproduced by permission (p. 22).

Christian Aid: from J. Morley, H. Ward and J. Wild, *Dear Life: Praying through the Year with Christian Aid*, 1998 (p. 56).

Christian Concern for One World: www.ccow.org.uk (p. 51).

Church Pastoral Aid Society: for Dick Williams (ed.) *Prayers for Today's Church*, 1972 (p. 81).

ECEN: from ECEN for Creation Time, 2008, copyright © Robin Morrison, 2006 (p. 54) and copyright © Eleanor Todd, 2007 (p. 55)

Fortress Press: from Arnold Kenseth, *Prayers for Worship Leaders*, 1978 (p. 42).

HarperCollins: from Angela Ashwin, *The Book of a Thousand Prayers*, 1986 (pp. 10, 11, 41, 62, 74).

International Peace Council: Desmond Tutu, 'Lord , how can I serve you?' (p. 43).

The Mothers' Union: from *The Mothers' Union Anthology of Public Prayers* (pp. 4, 63), reproduced with permission of The Mothers' Union, 24 Tufton Street, London SW1P 3RB; www.themothersunion.org

O Books: from Marcus Braybrooke (ed.), *One Thousand World Prayers*, 2003 (pp. 39, 65, 79).

Penguin Books: from Elizabeth Stuart (ed.), *Daring to Speak Love's Name*, Hamish Hamilton, 1992 (p. 25).

Randon House: from Henry Nouwen, *A Cry for Mercy*, Image Books, 2002 (p. 37).

SCM-Canterbury Press: from Caryl Micklem, *Contemporary Prayers for Public Worship*, copyright © Caryl Micklem 1967 (p. 39); Rex Chapman, *The Glory of God*, copyright © Rex Chapman 1974; used by permission.

SPCK: from David Adam, *The Edge of Glory*, 1985 (p. 4); *Tides and Seasons*, 1989 (p. 18); *The Cry of the Deer*, 1989 (p. 44); Janet Morley, *All Desires Known*, 1992 (pp. 6, 35, 55, 76); Kathy Keay, in John Pritchard (ed.), *The SPCK Book of Christian Prayer*, 2009 (p.30).

United Reformed Church: from Jean Mortimer, *Exceeding our Limits*, 1991 (pp. 48, 51).

Scripture quotations for the New Revised Standard Version (NRSV) are copyright © 1989, 1995 by the division of Christian Education of the National Council of Churches in the United States of America and used by permission.